HOW TO BUY, REHAB, AND RESELL

RESIDENTIAL PROPERTY:

All of My Best Tips

I0467499

By Jay Thomas

Copyright © 2015 by Jay Thomas

How to Buy, Rehab, and Resell Residential Property:

All of My Best Tips

Copyright © 2015 by Jay Thomas.

Cover Credit: Jay Thomas

TABLE OF CONTENTS

INTRODUCTION

This book is intended as a primer on how to buy, rehab, and resell residential properties. Those who have never rehabbed a property but who have a burning desire to do so will receive the most benefit from the text. However, even experienced rehabbers might find some value in it.

For over twenty years, I was a so-called "flipper"—a person who buys, rehabs, and resells residential properties. I prefer not to think of myself that way because I have seen plenty of flippers who did slipshod work and who had no qualms about selling that inferior product to end buyers. Their motto always seemed to be, "Good enough for who it's for." That might explain why certain properties tend to go into foreclosure over and over again. End buyers might feel as if everything about the property is not copacetic and decide to quit making their mortgage payments.

I and the partners I worked with had consciences and wanted the process to be a win-win for everyone involved. We wanted to do quality work, improve the property to its original state, or even beyond that, make a tidy profit, and sell the end buyers a property that they could be proud of owning.

Not using a level to check for both level and plumb on base kitchen cabinets, so that when countertops were laid on top of the cabinets there was a large gap between the top of the cabinets and the bottom of the countertops at one end, failing to install interior doors so that they were not dragging along on the new carpet, not using ground fault interrupting plugs in outlets near sources of water, failing to fix holes in walls created by door handles, and not using di-electric unions when connecting a new hot water heater to a copper piping system are only a few examples of the slipshod work I have seen performed by "flippers". I have seen even worse things that left me shaking my head in disbelief.

I once bought a property with a flipper at a foreclosure sale. The house burned before the sale and the financial institution was going to be opening the bidding at $6,000, even though the bid would have been for significantly more had the fire not occurred. The flipper suggested that we buy it together rather than competing with each other. We got it for $6,001. It was a larger than typical one story home for its subdivision with a full basement with its own outside entrance in an area where most homes were on either slabs or crawl spaces.

 The flipper's ideas about what to do with the property and mine were pretty far apart so I was willing to let him buy out my interest for $25,000. He thought it would be a snap to rehab-- but because of the fire, I knew the City's building inspectors would be all over who ever undertook the rehab. He took three quarters of a year working on it before he could put it up for resell. I shouldn't really say that he was working on it because he did not do any work himself—he had a crew of illegals run by a naturalized citizen. Two member of that crew were well below sixteen years of age.

It is my sincere hope that should you, the reader, get involved in buying, rehabbing and reselling residential properties that you will do it the correct way so that it is a win-win for you and for your future buyers.

Because I pride myself on thinking outside of the box and not being confined to a fixed way of doing things, I will say that I found and purchased properties in several different ways: foreclosure auctions, purchases through Realtors, purchase from someone who was in foreclosure, buying properties from someone who perfected a tax deed, as a result of a guaranteed sales contract, and as real estate owned from a financial institution. However, the majority of my purchases were at foreclosure auction sales. Additionally, not all of my properties were sold through Realtors and some were sold without undergoing complete rehabs, as you will read later.

I purchased one property from someone who was in foreclosure at the time, and I had two near misses. It is almost impossible to get to speak with people who are in the foreclosure process because most of them do not want to deal with the reality of the situation.

As far as the near misses, in one instance the husband who was living in the property agreed to sell but his ex-wife refused because she did not want to help him out of the situation. Even

9

when we explained to her that she would actually be helping herself because her credit rating as well as his would be hurt by the foreclosure, she could not bring herself to help the ex-husband. In the other instance, we convinced the woman to sell to us and we made her a special offer so that she would have not had to pay any prorations or other normal seller expenses. Her college student son talked her out of the deal and she wound up listing with a Realtor. She did sell her home before the foreclosure sale was scheduled, but the bottom line, for her, was that she netted $9,000 less than she would have had she sold her home to us.

My path into rehabbing.

How did I get into buying, rehabbing, and reselling residential properties? That is an interesting and complex question with several components. Let's say that I did not want to be in someone's employ, that I read a few books and took a few courses on real estate investing, and because I was a frustrated architect want to be. Why I did not study architecture in college is too long of a story to explore here. Although I have no traditional artistic ability, I was

10

excellent at mechanical drawing, loved studying blueprints, and have a distinct flair for redesigning bathrooms, kitchens, and other home components. Had I gone into traditional remodeling, I would not have had the freedom to design kitchens and bathrooms that I had as a rehabber, or as I prefer to think of it as a "Restorationist."

When I started out on this journey, I really did not know squat about rehabbing, which should be encouraging to those of you who want to do rehabbing but who are not certain that you have the skills necessary to do it. Beside hand tools, I owned one corded 3/8 inch drill and one corded circular saw. Cordless tools, which now dominate the tool market, were just beginning to appear in stores and catalogs (no websites were around then either). Fortunately, when I was taking my real estate course, I met a guy who had been a mechanic, roofer, handyman, and was assisting a heating and air conditioning contractor on jobs. He also wanted to get into rehabbing. We kept in contact and I began watching television shows like This Old House and Hometime. In those days, there was no DIY network or Home and Garden television. I also began reading magazines like, Taunton's Fine Homebuilding and Fine Woodworking, Fine Homebuilding's Kitchens and Baths, the Journal of Light Construction, American Woodworker, Better Homes & Gardens Wood Magazine, The Family Handyman, and others, most of them are available at bookstores like Barnes & Nobles and in your local library.

Nowadays, most, if not all, of the magazines are still available: additionally, there are others like This Old House Magazine, HGTV Magazine, Better Homes & Gardens Kitchen and Bath Makeovers, Better Homes & Gardens Kitchen and Bath Ideas, and Signature Kitchens and Baths. This Old House, both the television show and the magazine are still good sources as is the television show Ask This Old House. Hometime is far less hands on and is concentrating more on building upper scale homes, but you have Ron Hazelton, Knock It Off, and a slew of shows on cable networks that will show how to undertake and perform rehabbing tasks. I believe that there are plenty of videos on YouTube showing how to undertake and perform specific projects.

What you need to know.

Since all of the properties I dealt with were located in the suburbs surrounding Chicago, my comments are based on Illinois laws regarding foreclosure, and they might not be applicable in other states. If you are in a state other than Illinois, or even if you are in Illinois, I would advise you to check out the applicable laws and statues in your state. To begin that process, you should go to your local library and look through your state statute books to find the statutes pertaining to foreclosure. If your library does not have them, which is difficult to imagine, then you might try your local county courthouse because many of them contain law libraries. Next you might want to speak with the person or parties responsible for selling foreclosures in your area in order to make sure that you know exactly how the process works in your state. You might need to know how much money you need to have with you in order to bid, what form of payment they prefer, when you need to bring in the balance, when the sale gets confirmed, when you can take possession of the property, what process you need to go through in order to

13

evict the previous owners, if they do not voluntarily move out of the property, and anything else you need to clarify. Issues like these are some of the things that can vary from state to state.

In most states, you will require the services of an attorney to handle the paperwork for your closings when you resell the properties. You should not need their services when you purchase properties from foreclosure auctions. If you are purchasing properties through other sources, then you might require an attorney to handle your closing. I did not suggest seeking the advice of an attorney when researching out the foreclosure process in your state because most attorneys are not well versed in the intricacies of the foreclosure process and you will wind up paying them for their time so that they can learn what you need to know. Around the country there are law firms which specialize in handling foreclosures for banks and other financial institutions. There is a chance that you might be able to get some information about the process from an attorney working for a so-called "foreclosure mill." If you attend the sales and the confirmation hearings you might get one of them to discuss foreclosure in general with you and it may only cost you the price of a cup of Starbucks coffee.

Good luck to you, if you decide to proceed. This book should provide some nuggets of information that will help you in your efforts.

One. Education.

Perhaps it is only me, but I have always thought of rehabbing as an occupation that should involve continuing education. There are others in the field who know a certain way of doing things and they will keep doing it that way until the end of time. They are the personification of a quote from Abraham Maslow, "If the only tool you have is a hammer, you are likely to perceive every problem as a nail."

I realized early on that new products and new tools are being developed on a continual basis and that only by educating oneself can one keep abreast of the newest products and latest techniques for performing certain rehabbing tasks.

I not only perused publications to keep on top of things, I attended JLC Live Events, when they were held in the Midwest (in Columbus, Ohio, Indianapolis, Indiana, and Minneapolis, Minnesota), the Remodeling Show, when it was held in the Midwest (in Indianapolis, Indiana and Chicago, Illinois), several Katz Roadshows events, which were held at various lumber yards,

16

and Berland's House of Tools Labor Day Events (until they quit having them), which is where I met Scott Phillips of the American Woodshop PBS show and Steve Thomas, the former host of the This Old House PBS show. I have learned both time tested and modern techniques from the likes of Mike Sloggatt, Gary Katz, Rick Arnold, Myron Ferguson, Scott Phillips, Mike Guertin, Frank Caputo, Greg Burnet, and many others.

If it were not for the efforts I took to educate myself, I would not have known the value of capped PVC products like Azek, which can be used not only outside of the property but inside as well—as trim around windows in bathrooms and kitchens. Capped PVC products can be used to replace deteriorated wooden decking boards, which I did once and for exterior trim.

I learned how to install crown molding, the best way to install a pre-hung door, how to best install kitchen cabinets, the best practices for installing replacement windows, how to hang and tape drywall efficiently, the pros and cons of different insulation products, and how to properly install Schulter Systems products to ensure getting a watertight and leak-proof bathroom shower and tub.

If you want to know about the latest and greatest techniques, products, and tools, you must make a sincere effort to educate yourself by attending workshops and talking with company representatives.

Each individual aspect of rehabbing has its own tricks and techniques, which you have to pick up from somewhere or someone. Neophyte drywall mudders tend to use too much compound rather than too little, beginning plumbers tend to use too much solder on copper pipe connections and forget that horizontal drain pipe needs a downward pitch, and first-time window and door installers often fail to realize the value of plumb and level.

Two. The Realtor Question.

Are you a Realtor? If not, do you have a friend or a relative who is a Realtor? If not, then you are going to have to find a Realtor or become a Realtor.

Do you know how to find one? It seems a bit of a foolish question because there are Realtors in offices all around your geographical area. However, you don't want just any Realtor—you want one who is going to understand what you are seeking to do and who is willing to give you some of his or her time, realizing that eventually you are going to be giving them listings. In real estate they have a saying, "You have to list to last."

Before I give you some tips about finding your Realtor, I am going to suggest that you take a course in order to get your own real estate license. Some real estate offices and local community colleges offer the course you have to take in order to take and pass your state's real estate license test. Even if you do not take the test to obtain your real estate license, you will have people in your course who are going to

19

take the examination and who are going to become Realtors. You will have an opportunity to get to know some of them, even if they may not be the ideal candidate you are seeking to serve as your Realtor.

Say you take and past your state examination and are now a Realtor, do you really want to be an active real estate agent or do you simply want to warehouse your license. Some, but not all, real estate offices will allow you to warehouse your license. If you tell the broker or owner of the office what you are planning to do, he or she might be interested in allowing you to warehouse your license there because you will eventually be creating listings for their office.

One advantage of having your real estate license, even if you are not seeking to be a full-time Realtor is that when you list your properties for sale, you can list them and part of the commission will come back to you when the property sells. Before I made the move into buying, rehabbing, and reselling residential properties, I was a Realtor and even acquired my Broker-Associate license. My one regret is that I let my license lapse. In Illinois, at that time, all

Realtors were legally considered to be agents of the Sellers and could not legally represent the interests of Buyers (even though some unethical ones did). Had I known that the state was going to change the regulations and allow Realtors to represent Buyers, I would have kept my license.

Now, if the thought of obtaining your own real estate license holds no interest for you, then you need to find one who will work with you. The best way to do that might be to search for any real estate investor groups in your area, like the Chicago Creative Investors Association, mentioned later in this book, and see if you can find a real estate agent who is either a member of the group or who advertises his or her services through such a group. That Realtor will have a better idea about what you are aiming to do and are unlikely to be continually bothering you with listings that do not meet your qualifications.

I cannot even begin to tell you how many times I have had Realtors tell me about a property that they thought would be ideal for me; and when I asked them for details about it, they would tell me it could sell for $100,000 and I could get it for $90,000. Just to humor them, I would ask what the property needed and they would say something like: new appliances, new carpeting, and extensive painting. I would then have to explain that $100,000 minus the normal six percent real estate commission left only $94,000; and deducting the cost of appliances, carpet, and painting from that left little or nothing for me. I would then have to explain to them, once again, that if I could get it for around $70,000 to $80,000 that I might be interested in looking at the property.

No matter how many Realtors you explain your requirements to, many are not going to understand what you are saying—that is why it is better to find one who belongs to an investment group or who advertises there.

The most prolific real estate agents are usually not good choices because they are so busy that they are going to see you as a waste of their good time. If they do not see some reward from giving you their time fairly quickly, they are going to give you less and less of their time. Eventually, they will neither answer nor return your calls.

In my years of buying, rehabbing, and reselling residential property, I only ever found one Realtor who completely comprehended what I was all about. I found two or three others who got the idea sufficiently that I could work with them and they did not waste my time telling me about frivolous properties that did not meet my requirements.

When you have a property ready to be listed, you should tell your Realtor that you want them to have all Realtors showing the property to contact them to schedule a showing and that you want to be informed about each and every showing. Why? Because the property will be essentially vacant and you want to make certain that it is as secure as possible. Either you or your Realtor should check on the property once a week at the bare minimum. I remember one property that was shown and the Realtor, who showed it, did not even close the front door or turn off the lights that should have been turned off. The storm door was closed but the lock box was on the handle of the actual front door and that door was wide open. And that could have led to the house being vandalized.

23

Then there is the issue of lights being turned on that you do not want on, lights being turned off that you do want on, blinds or drapes being opened when you do not want them opened, furnace or air conditioning thermostat settings being changed, faucets not being completely shut off, and a list of other things as well.

Another option is to make friends, if you can do so, with one or more of the neighbors. Give them your phone number and ask them to give you a call, if they see anything suspicious or out of order at the property.

Nowadays, if you have a smart phone and if you are willing to spend a couple of hundred dollars for the equipment, you can purchase a system, such as those described later in this book, that will send you picture of anyone who comes to the front door of the property. You could even speak with them as well, which might be very helpful if the potential buyer has any questions about the property.

Until you familiarize yourself with values in your chosen area, a good Realtor is worth his or her weight in gold if they know the area you are concentrating in, if they know values in that area and can tell you what a particular property would resell for, and if they are willing to take your calls when you need them and not bother you when you do not.

Three. Falling in Love

Falling in love with a property can only lead to heartbreak. Every time I have seen someone fall in love with a property it has not turned out well. I can actually speak from personal experience here since the last house I bought was one I fell in love with and it was the only property on which I ever lost money. But I have had to fight the feeling off a few times and I have seen other investors make crucial mistakes because they fell in love with a property. The biggest crucial mistake is paying too much for a property so that you cannot possibly turn a profit on it. You are most likely to fall in love with a property when you have no property you are currently working on and when it has been awhile since you have purchased one.

Remember, you are not going to be living there. This is only an investment for you and should be treated as such. Every decision should be a rationally thought out decision. You must always be prepared to walk away from any property and if you get into a bidding war with other interested parties, do not exceed the maximum price limit you have established in your mind in advance of the auction. You might be able to get away with going slightly over your preordained price but only if you are doing so to see if the other bidders will drop out of the bidding.

If you do not get that particular property, there are going to be others coming along, which may turn out to be better deals for you.

The two best deals I could have had but never got were two townhomes, owned by the same person; they sold at the foreclosure auction for a combined total of $8,500. I let a Sherriff's deputy talk me into not bidding because he did not like the subdivision in which they were located. Yes, it was not the best area but it was not as bad as he thought. Rehabbed the two would have sold for $143,000 easily and I could have made an easy $100,000 profit. The moral of the story is to listen to your own thoughts and not the prejudices of others when it comes to purchasing properties.

Remember that everybody has to live somewhere and even though you would not want to live there, does not mean that you won't be able to resell the property. So, don't hate a property just because you do not like where it is located.

There are reasons why someone might fall in love with a property: they like the style of the property, they like the neighborhood in which it is located, and several more. Usually, it is a love at first sight thing but it can be a long-term affair because you may have always been fascinated by this particular property and when it becomes available, your long-smoldering affection for it flares up.

No property is that much of a gem that rationality can yield to emotionality and have everything turn out well. The bottom line is that buying, rehabbing, and reselling residential properties is a business—plain and simple.

28

Four. Never Assume...Unless

Never assume that because the homeowner is maintaining the property on the outside and has attractive landscaping, that the interior is well maintained. I have seen it several times and as they say, "you cannot judge a book by its cover."

I purchased a home at a foreclosure auction and about a month before the auction the owner was painting the outside of the two story home. It was well landscaped as well and I assumed that he must have been maintaining the inside. That assumption could not have been further from the truth. He hadn't known that the home was in foreclosure because his wife was keeping it secret from him. The inside could have used some of his attention because in the ten plus years that they had been living there, he had not done a thing to the inside of the property.

Never assume that you have researched the property well enough. You either know that you have or you need to go back and make sure that you have all the information you need. I created a checklist type document to keep track of the

29

information that I had or did not have about any particular property.

It is extremely rare that you would find a large VA mortgage in second position on a property, but it can happen. At one sheriff's sale, a property with an end value of approximately $220,000 had an opening bid of $105,000. There were several parties bidding and the winning bid was just shy of $120,000. None of the usual bidders were bidding because they knew that there was an $85,000 first mortgage and the mortgagee's position was safe and not eradicated by the sale because it was in the first position. The successful bidding group found this out immediately after the sale, and they were able to get the bidder who finished second in the bidding to assume their position so that they did not lose any money nor did they make any money but they were happy to be out from under the obligation of purchasing the property. The party who had been second in the bidding did not know the truth of the matter and the winning bidder felt no responsibility to inform them about the situation.

Never assume that the owners who lost their property at a sheriff's sale will leave all of the light fixtures, appliances, and cabinetry behind, if they are still living in the property at the time of the sale or even if they moved out of the property just before the sale took place. In a significant number of cases, whether the homes were under $100,000 in value or over $500,000 in value, I have either seen or heard about homes where the former owner(s) took everything they could detach from the structure.

In one instance, the man losing his house cut through all of the floor joists and in a matter of months, the first floor sank about four feet into the basement. When you walked into the front door, there was a small area where you could safely stand; then you could look into the kitchen and see all of the cabinetry attached to the walls with no floor holding them up.

If you do make any assumptions, assume that the condition of the property will be even worse than you think because if it is not, then you will feel relieved.

Five. Pick Your Price and Stick to It.

When you are considering buying a property at an auction, especially a sheriff's sale, you are essentially buying a pig in a poke, unless you have been able to get inside the property to make a decent appraisal of its condition. In those situations, I would never pay more than sixty percent of its resell value.

For example, you have determined that a particular house would be worth $100,000 all fixed up; then I would not be willing to pay more than $60,000 for it. If the opening bid were for, say, $105,000, then I would not bid on it. If the opening bid were going to be $45,000, then I would be willing to bid to $60,000.

Because plaintiff's in foreclosure cases will sometimes underbid their position, you have to prepare as if that will be the case, even if it turns out not to be so. The bottom line is that you set your upper limit bid in advance of the sale and you do not change it. If the bidding goes past your limit, you simply shrug your shoulders and know that other properties will be coming up for sale, if not that particular day, then sometime in the future.

I have seen many bidders who did not have discipline and they usually screwed themselves because they either did not have a realistic appraisal of the property's resale value, they were way off base on their projected rehab costs, or they got into a bidding war mentality and kept on bidding even though they should have known better and stopped. When you do that often enough, you will not be buying properties over a long period of time.

I purchased several properties at auctions because no one bid against me. There were second mortgages on the properties but they did not attend the auction to bid their position. If that happens then the second mortgage and anything mortgages or liens beyond that are eradicated.

For me to exceed my sixty percent figure, I had to positively know that I could still make a decent return by bidding to sixty-five or seventy percent of the projected resell value, and I did do that a few times—very few.

Six. The Taking of Title.

You have to think about how you want to take the title to the property, whether you buy it from a foreclosure sale, from a financial institution's real estate owned department, through a Realtor, or any other means.

You can take it in your name only, if you have no partners, as joint tenants, if you do have a partner, as tenants in common, if you have one or more partners, in the name of your business or corporation, or in a land trust. The most secure method is to take title in a land trust which you would have to have established in advance of the sale or closing, if you buy it through a Realtor or from an estate.

A land trust is secure in the sense of protecting your privacy and giving you options for selling the property that are not available in any other method. In Illinois, land trusts can be set up through attorneys or through some banks. Usually the fees you will pay to the bank are less expensive than what you would pay to an attorney. This is something that you will want to check out for your particular state if you do not dwell in Illinois.

I had one partner who served as the funder on some purchases and who always took title in his name. Most of the property I purchased with my other partner was taken in title to a land trust created through a bank.

If you have an attorney, especially one you have the utmost confidence in, you can discuss how you might want to take title to any properties you purchase. If you either do not have an attorney or you are not that confident in his advice, you might go to a Real Estate Investment Club (which will be the subject of Chapter Eight) and see if any attorneys are members or advertise their services through the club. If neither of those things happen, then you could seek referrals from other members about attorneys.

Seven. Insurance is a Necessity.

If you are the successful bidder at an auction, make certain that you have insurance on the property as of that day, if at all possible.

In many states, like Illinois, the successful bidder technically owns the property after the sale, even though they may not get immediate possession of the property. To be perfectly honest the successful bidder does not actually own the property until the confirmation of the sale, which is normally about one week later. Technically, the judge could void the sale if something happens or comes to light during that period.

I had that happen one time to me. It was a deal in which I was partnering with the funder. The attorney representing a party who bought the property from the previous owner and the title company claimed that the sale was completed before the auction took place. They could produce no specific time dated documentation to show that it occurred that way and the judge who overturned the sale encouraged my funder to challenge his decision by appealing, but the

36

funder chose not to appeal, which I, to this day, still feel was a blunder on the funder's part.

In Illinois, the previous homeowner, if they are residing in the home at the time of the sale, will have thirty days from the confirmation date to voluntarily vacate the property or put themselves in the position to be evicted.

A partner and I purchased a property and I obtained an insurance policy that went into effect on the confirmation day; two days later, the former homeowners, who were no longer in residence at the time of the sale, burned the property because they mistakenly thought that they could collect on their homeowner's insurance policy which was still in effect (only because their insurance provider did not know that they had lost the home) and that my partner and I would not suffer financially because the court would give us back our money. Had they done it before the confirmation they may well have been correct.

The property had a huge hole through the roof was basically a total loss and the previous homeowners were guilty of arson.

37

Unfortunately, for my partner and I, the insurance company's claims people put us through hell. Initially, they were suspicious that we set the fire, then they did not want to pay out the claim because they thought that we purchased the home below market value, which was true, if it had been in pristine condition, which it was not. Also, the holder of the second mortgage on the property did not show up to bid its position. Had that happened the property would have sold for in excess of $130,000 and we would not have bid on it.

We should have been able to collect up to $115,000 (which was the figure that the insurance company had come up with for homes in that particular subdivision when I took the policy out) and they tried to get us to accept $52,000 because they found a contractor who they said would replace the home for that amount. As I told them, I had a Ford before the fire and a Ford was what I wanted after the property was restored. I was not looking for a Mercedes but neither was I willing to accept a Yugo.

They tried their best to screw us out of financial provisions for landscaping and other things as well. Eventually, we found a fire restoration company which was run by a couple of former insurance company employees (not the same company we were battling) and let them go at it with our insurance company. They had to prepare a bid but theirs was thirty pages long as compared to the half page bid made by the insurance company's stooge. The insurance company had to accept the bid of my contractors because they knew that they could never win in court—which is where I was threatening to go if they did not.

At the end, we wound up with a completely new property, which our insurance paid for to the tune of $114,000. Because everything was new and improved, we wound up selling it for almost $150,000—the highest sale price of any home in that particular neighborhood ever. My partner and I made out like bandits (figuratively speaking) because we only paid $81,000 for the property at the sale and the insurance company paid for rebuilding (or rehabbing) it.

The moral is that even though the chances of a fire like this happening are slim would you rather sleep easy at night or be worried that your investment could turn into a pile of ashes.

Eight. Real Estate Investment Clubs.

If you live in or near a metropolitan area, like I do by being in the Chicago suburbs, it would be in your best interest to find a real estate investment club to join. The REIClub.com (www.reiclub.com) web site has a state-by-state listing of nearly 300 real estate investing clubs. There are six listings for the state of Illinois.

I belonged to the Chicago Creative Investors Association, which is the oldest and largest of the groups in metropolitan Chicago. Jane Garvey has been running the club since before I ever got involved in real estate and she is a major player on the national level and is very involved in legislative efforts in the state of Illinois. CCIA holds monthly meetings with an outside speaker each meeting as well as bringing in nationally-known experts to present classes on specialized training on real estate investing issues.

They have a per-meeting rate, if you only want to attend certain monthly meetings, or you can save money by purchasing a yearly dues plan. It is fifteen dollars per meeting, if you are not a

41

member, and $99 per year if you are. There is an even bigger discount if two people share a membership.

Not all of the members are going to be interested in your particular form of investment—most are going to be landlords, some are going to be Realtors looking to sell property or to find investors to work with (remember, I mentioned this might be a way to find yourself a Realtor, if you do not already have one), some are going to be people with money who are looking for people to do the labor on rehab projects, and some are going to be rehabbers who need a money source. There may be others with other investment interests as well.

These real estate investment clubs may be a place for you to find recommendations for people with specific skills (carpet installers, HVAC professionals, roofers, plumbers, electricians, tree cutters, etc.) to assist you with your rehab projects. Because so many members are landlords, they have had the need to hire some of those professionals from time to time.

42

There are other advantages in joining a real estate investment club because many of them have arranged for members to get discounts from stores such as Home Depot, Sherwin Williams, OfficeMax, and many others.

Like I said, networking with other club members may pay great dividends and you will be exposed to other forms of real estate investing, which will broaden your perspective.

Nine. The Tools You Need.

If you are going to be rehabbing properties, then you or a partner, and you will need a partner because it is too costly to pay building professionals to rehab properties for you, are going to have to have some tools. There are certain basic tools you will need and there are specialty tools, like jack hammers and floor sanders, that you can rent, if you ever have a need for them.

If you need to purchase tools, you can do so from Amazon (www.amazon.com), Acme Tools (www.acmetool.com), Tool Barn (www.toolbarn.com), CPO Outlet Tool Stores (www.cpoutlets.com), Tyler Tool Outlet (www.tylertool.com) the big box stores (like Menard's, Lowe's, and Home Depot), or tool stores, like Berland's House of Tools with three locations in the Chicagoland area. A tool store generally carries a broader spectrum of tools than the big box stores do. If you want to go the low cost route, there is always Harbor Freight tools, which has both a web site and retail stores all around the country.

Beside the standard screwdrivers, wrenches, pliers, pry bars, chisels, hammers, measuring tapes, files, wood rasps, and such, you are going to need a variety of electric and/or battery-powered tools:

A reciprocating saw,

A 3/8 inch drill/driver,

A ¼ inch impact driver,

A right angle drill,

A variable speed random orbit sander,

A jig saw (D handle or barrel grip),

A 3 1/4 inch planer,

A portable jobsite table saw,

A multi-piece oscillating tool,

A compound or dual compound miter saw,

A drywall cutting tool,

A router,

A circular saw.

A handheld grinder.

Be warned, if you are not familiar with power tools, that they are all potentially dangerous, so work safely, wear the proper safety googles and hearing protection (especially around the louder tools), and keep your mind focused on what you are doing.

While all of them are potentially dangerous, the most dangerous tool is the table saw. I once got into an argument with a fellow, at a Rockler store, about the most dangerous tool; he thought it was the router and I thought it was the table saw. I saw that he had a couple of mangled fingers and I asked him if he got those from a router accident—he said no, he got them from a table saw accident. I have known at least four people who have gotten injured by a piece of wood coming off of a table saw. I myself have almost been hit twice. Caution is the word, especially when working with table saws.

With respect to a circular saw, I would recommend purchasing a worm drive or what they call a sidewinder, if you are right handed, because then you can track the cut of the blade better.

As far as routers go, smaller, less powerful ones only can be used with ¼ inch shank bits whereas the larger, more powerful units can be used with both ¼ inch and ½ inch bits, which gives you more flexibility and a wider variety of bits from which to choose. Some are fixed base and some are plunge routers. Plunge routers are considered easier to use but which kind you want depends on your personal preference.

The main reason you need a right angle drill is to screw cabinets together. Only a right angle drill can get into the small drawer space of smaller base cabinets, or into smaller base or wall cabinets. You will be able to use it in other applications as well.

You are also going to need 24 inch, 48 inch, and 72 inch levels. As master carpenter, Gary Katz, would tell you, use the largest level you have for the job. The 72 inch level is primarily for plumbing doors. When purchasing a level, confirm its accuracy by checking its level on one side and then turning it over and seeing if the reading is the same. You may also want to have some sort of laser level, particularly for laying out kitchen cabinets.

With cordless tools, you can often find deal packages where you get multiple tools and batteries for a reduced price over what you would pay if the items were purchased separately. The companies that offer the widest selection of tools are Bosch, Craftsman, DeWalt, Festool, Hitachi, Makita, Milwaukee, Porter-Cable, Ridgid, and Ryobi. Ryobi tools are the least expensive of this bunch. Festool is like the Ferrari of the tool world in that some of their designs are different and they are definitely more expensive than the other brands. The brand is manufactured in Germany and is of extremely high quality. The Festool jig saw uses a thicker blade than the other brands do, which means that the blades have to fit the Festool jig saw and you cannot use the commonly available brands.

Metabo, Panasonic, Dremel, Black & Decker, Rockwell, Drill Master, Skil, Tradespro, Kawasaki, Chicago Power, Performax, ToolShop, Masterforce, Wen, Ingersoll Rand, and Worx, among others, have some tools but not a complete range of them. You can sometimes find factory reconditioned tools from the top name brands and purchase them for less than the full retail price but with the same warranty. I have several factory reconditioned tools and have never had a problem with any of them.

For years, I used a Delta 10 inch bench saw, a work site table saw, with a few accessories which I purchased for a reasonable price and never really had any problem with it other than it being somewhat problematic for cutting larger stock, before I moved up to a Bosch 4000 10 inch table saw.

You might also be able to find some excellent deals on Ebay (www.ebay.com) or on Craigslist (www.craigslist.org)

As I have mentioned elsewhere in this text, the more expensive brand name tools are made better and made to last longer under heavy usage. That does not mean that you need to purchase more expensive tools to begin rehabbing properties—you can get by with less expensive tools until and unless you can see that the need is there for tools of higher quality.

49

Additionally, you are going to need a five gallon or larger shop vacuum, several work lights, several Bessey or Irwin clamps, Pony Cabinet Claws (clamps designed for aligning the fronts of wall and base cabinets when you are setting them in place), a Collins Coping Foot (designed for specific jig saw models), a T-Jak or other support for holding wall cabinets when setting them in place, a fifty foot fish tape for pulling electrical wire through walls (if you are in an area where they do not require that all electrical wiring be inside of conduit), an electric outlet tester, an electric presence sensor, several drywall taping knives in three or four different sizes, a Goldblatt Blade Runner and other tools for cutting drywall, a three or four piece set of nail sets for finishing nails, a grout float, notched trowels, a tile nibbler, a tile and grout brush, a variety of other tiling tools, several sizes of hole saws, a Little Giant ladder or a knockoff version of the Little Giant (because it is the most versatile ladder on the market and it can replace several other ladders), and, maybe, a Cadex 23 gauge pneumatic pin nailer, or its equivalent, for assembling moldings. Calculated Industries makes several calculators; the Construction

Master Pro is a wonder for rehabbers and construction professionals. Mike Slogatt, at a JLC live event, is the one who introduced me to its value for construction applications. This was not meant to be an exhaustive listing. It is meant to give you an idea about the variety of tools you are going to need when doing rehabbing.

Every year the folks at Fine Homebuilding, Fine Woodworking, Pro Tool Reviews (www.protoolreviews.com), Better Homes & Gardens Wood Magazine (www.woodmagazine.com), and some of the other woodworking magazines as well as Tools of the Trade magazine (www.toolsofthetrade.net), and Power Tools Wizard (www.powertoolswizard.com) compile a list of tools available and make recommendations as to which are best, based on several categories of performance. Those sources would be a good place to start if you are seeking to expand the array of tools in your arsenal for rehabbing residential properties.

You may well find that you need more than the power tools I have recommended you possess but what I have listed will cover ninety percent

51

of the day in and day out work you will
encounter in rehabbing

Ten. Never Over Improve the Property.

You are not going to be living there and things that you might like in your personal residence may not be appropriate in the rehabbed home and, even worse, may not get you any more money from the eventual buyer. For instance, a new $150 front door, if needed, might be similar to what all of the other homes in that price range have and while an $800 front door might look better and be of much better quality, you are really not going to get an extra $650 in your resell price. The same thing is true of putting a whirlpool tub in a home where none of its real estate comparables have one.

Types of improvements that can reap dividends include adding another bathroom, improving the kitchen or bathroom layouts, reducing the number of doorways into a kitchen, replacing old, drafty windows with new, energy efficient ones—even if they are not the top of the line new windows—putting a working garage door opener in a garage.

When it comes to things like installing new lighting fixtures, which I am a big proponent of

53

doing, just make sure that you are not installing fixtures in a $100,000 home that would be more appropriate in a $500,000 home. If you have any questions about appropriateness, your Realtor should be able to take you to see some listings in your projected resell range, so that you can settle the matter in your own mind. After you have been rehabbing for a few years, you should have a pretty good idea about appropriateness and not have to go and look at properties to confirm your feelings.

Improving the property is a good thing but over improving it may help you to sell it faster but, as a general rule, it will really not help your bottom line.

Eleven. Cheaper is Not Always Better.

Years ago, I worked in a plant, for one long summer, where we made and packaged pancake mixes among other things. One of my jobs was to glue labels on bags which were then filled with mix. It was funny to read all of these labels extolling the virtues of each brand's product and the awards they had been given when one knew that they were each getting the same product as everyone else. I suppose in the process of making batter, companies had leeway to alter the wet ingredients which could have made a difference.

When you see the same mix going into a variety of bags you begin to think that cheaper is better because you are getting the same thing but for less money. However, the cheapest cabinets from any big box store are decidedly inferior to the cabinets that are more expensive. Think plain joint drawers versus dovetail joints and thinner material rather than something more substantial.

I would never use the cheapest cabinets from a big box store in any rehab project of mine. Even

55

in my lowest priced resells, I have only gone down to about three price points above their rock bottom priced cabinets. In my opinion, the lowest priced cabinets only have two uses: to be used in a rental property in a bad area where one does not want to invest heavily or in one's basement workshop where they will never be seen.by anyone outside of your family.

Because of my long ago work experience, I had thought that the difference between a $79 router and a $299 router was minimal at best and that most of the price difference had to do with Brand Names. I was mistaken. Not only do better materials go into the more expensive router but it also has a motor made to give you many more hours of running time. I have had a couple of well-known carpenters and woodworkers explain to me how the $79 router may give you ten to fifteen hours of actual running time whereas the $299 one may give you one hundred and fifty to two hundred hours of running time. The cheaper one probably only accepts quarter inch router bits while the more expensive router can accept both quarter inch and half inch bits.

If your experience would be the same as mine, you could probably get by with a cheaper router rather than a more expensive one. If you were either planning on making many board feet of your own moldings or making your own custom cabinetry, then you would probably be better served by buying a more expensive router.

The same process can be applied to any power tool you might think you are going to need in carrying out your rehab work—table saw, reciprocating saw, jig saw, circular saw, drill/driver, impact driver, and planer. It is more expensive because of how it is made and what goes into it but that does not mean that you need to have the most expensive tools to do quality work.

Twelve. New Does Not Mean Expensive.

I have said it previously, but I want to reiterate it here again, "New does not necessarily mean expensive." It can be but only if it is appropriate for the resell price of the property. If you have a lower priced property, you do not have to purchase the most expensive fixtures, appliances, cabinetry, countertops, and so on. New, no matter how much the item costs, means the same thing to prospective buyers, but buyers in higher price ranges expect better quality items.

Over the course of replacing many toilets, we found a model by Crane that we really like because it was economically priced and it worked really well. We called it the "the flushing devil" because it functioned better than many models from other manufacturers with a loftier price tag.

Whether you are replacing appliances, windows, doors, lighting fixtures, countertops, cabinetry, toilets, bathtubs, plumbing fixtures, or carpeting you can find a variety of pricing and can choose the items that are most appropriate for the resell price of the property you own and are rehabbing.

There are refrigerators priced from $400 to $15,000 and if you have to replace one in a $100,000 property, you should be buying one at the lower end of that spectrum rather than at the higher end. The upper end properties can appropriately have Wolf ovens and Sub Zero refrigerators, but it would be foolish to spend that sort of money for appliances in a $100,000, $200,000, $300,000, or even $400,000 property. After you have been doing rehabs for a few years, you should have a fairly good sense of what is and what is not economically appropriate for the property you are preparing for resell.

Thirteen. New Appliances.

It is going to be very, very rare to find new or almost new appliances in any foreclosure that you purchase; in fact, it is going to be rare to find appliances that are reasonably clean. If the property has used appliances, you can almost count on the fact that you are going to have to clean them—and that can be a very odious process. I once spent two and half days attempting to clean an oven/range and that overwhelming process made me realize that new appliances are far more attractive than partially clean ones.

If you have a property that will be at the bottom of the resell pyramid, you might be able to get away without putting new appliances in the property if you can find used but very clean ones. Some cities have businesses that sell new and used appliances and I have put some used appliances in two properties that I was rehabbing.

While new appliances may not get you substantially more of a resell price, they should help the property to sell faster. Psychologically speaking, buyers like knowing that they Fare going to be the first to be using any new appliances.

The appliances you purchase should match or fit your property. Don't buy a gourmet stove and a refrigerator with all the bells and whistles for a property that will sell for $100,000. A normal thirty inch wide stove, even without self-cleaning and other features, will be greatly appreciated as long as it is new and clean. On the other hand, you may need the gourmet stove in a $500.000 property. That is when you can think about buying a Sub Zero refrigerator or a Wolf oven or you may choose to buy slightly less expensive, although still considered gourmet, brands.

Never underestimate the allure of new appliances, new plumbing fixtures, new countertops, and new kitchen and bathroom cabinetry in reselling residential properties.

Fourteen. New Plumbing Fixtures.

You know how some old faucets get that scratched up and crusty look? Everybody does. That is why new faucets in bathrooms and the kitchen as well as new toilets and, possibly, new bathtubs can help resell the property. If you think you can get by without replacing a bathtub, you well might be able to as long as it looks good, is well caulked, and you have a new toilet, faucet, and sink.

Remember that new does not have to equate with expensive. And even though you may want something nicer in your home, this is not your home and you are only seeking to improve it to the level of expectations for similarly priced homes.

I once purchased a seven year old home at a foreclosure sale. The property was worth over $450,000 after it was rehabbed. The hall bathroom on the second floor had a full size bath/shower combination, but someone must have been real frisky in the tub because almost the entire back wall of the tile surround had to be replaced due to the grouting being cracked so

62

severely about three and a half feet above the floor of the tub that when anybody took a shower, the water would go through the crack and through the drywall behind the crack, which was also cracked, and would up staining the ceiling of the formal living room which was directly below on the main floor. The tiles had to be meticulously cleaned, new drywall, and some new wood had to be installed to shore up the wall there. I cannot tell you what happened after the property was resold but I would not think that something similar occurred due to all of the bracing that was placed in the wall.

Now, had I known about Schluter Systems products at the time, I definitely would have used one or more of their products to ensure that such a thing did not happen again. I would urge you to find out everything you can about Schluter Systems and their various products. When properly installed, the Schluter Systems products will create a waterproof bathroom, whether it is used in a free standing shower, in a combination tub and shower, under a tile floor, or behind a tile wall. The products might be a bit pricey but they are definitely worth every

63

dime you will spend on them. For more information on the complete line of Schluter Systems products you can go to www.schluter.com Wedi is another company focusing on making waterproof products for bathroom installations. I personally do not think of their line quite as highly as I do of Schluter's but that could merely be personal preference. To find out more about Wedi and its products you can go to www.wedicorp.com

Fifteen. An Improved Kitchen Layout and New Countertops.

Some kitchen layout improvements are relatively minor and some are monumental. Taking out a doorway in order to make a straight galley kitchen into an "L" and moving around appliances in order to wind up with four times more cabinet space and counter space is fairly monumental. Putting in a microwave cabinet in order to get a microwave off of the countertop, thus freeing up countertop space is fairly minor.

Since most buyers are couples, the more attractive you can make the kitchen, within economic reason, the easier it is to sell the property and the more likely it is you will get close to your asking price, if it is priced correctly. I can honestly say that I have never purchased a property that could not use a little kitchen makeover.

The vast majority of countertops in this country are manufactured of a laminate material by manufacturers such as Formica, Wilsonart, Pionite, Nevamar, or Arborite. There are many colors and patterns available in this type of material and it is relatively inexpensive compared to solid surface materials like Corian or natural stone products (like granite, slate, and marble) or quartz composites; and you do not have to worry about potentially fortifying the floor to hold the weight of laminate countertops. Since there were probably Formica-like countertops in place when you purchased the property, you can assume that they were neither new nor well cared for and that they will have to be replaced. The chances of running across natural stone or quartz composite counters is rare until you approach $400.000 properties. You might start seeing Corian-type materials when you are purchasing a property in the middle $200,000s or higher.

In addition to the materials mentioned already, you might find countertops made from bamboo, from paper, from butcher block, from solid glass, from recycled glass, from scrap metal, from stainless steel, from ceramic or other tile, or from concrete. There are usually several sources from which you can find out about these materials.

66

If you should happen to acquire one of those properties where more expensive countertops have already been installed, there is a chance you will not have to replace what is there unless they are either dated or very poorly maintained. I have only had to replace countertops in such a property one time and I chose a quartz composite material (like DuPont's Zodiaq, Cambria, Consentino, Silestone, CeasarStone, Legacy, TechniStone, and Avanza) because natural stone does not come with warranties and if the stone breaks or cracks, you will replace it out of your pocket.

Quartz composites do not require annual or semi-annual sealing, they will not stain, they have more consistency in color and pattern than purely natural products, they seldom break (and are warrantied if they do), and all quartz composite countertops are considered to be anti-microbial. Many interior designers are now recommending quartz composite countertops to their customers rather than natural stone products.

It is a definite plus to be able to state that certain things (like kitchen cabinets, appliances, countertops, and fixtures) in the property are new.

As far as layout goes, there are numerous publications showing what prevailing thoughts are at that moment about kitchen layout and design. If designing kitchens and baths is not your forte, as it was mine, you could always bring your spouse or a female friend to the property and ask for suggestions. Women usually have a better understanding of what should go where because they spend more time in the kitchen than men do. The other alternative is to find someone amongst your friends and acquaintances who has had their kitchen or bathrooms remodeled. If you do not have such a party within your circle of acquaintances, then maybe you should ask your Realtor if he or she can put you in touch with someone who has had such a remodel.

Sixteen. Lighting.

New lighting is always an attractive sales point. I would evaluate what the status of the lighting in the property was when I acquired it and if I thought it needed better lighting, my first thought would be to put new fan lights in the bedrooms, living room, family room (if the property had one), and eating area.

Some houses require chandeliers rather than fan lights and your best bet, if that is the case, is to go to a local lighting store and find chandeliers that coordinate with each other and that are within your budget.

As far as fan lights go, you can purchase them for less than $100 or you buy them for over $1,000. It is another case of finding ones that are appropriate in your expected resell price range.

You will probably also have to be thinking about under cabinet, and even within the cabinet, lighting. New LED options are space saving and provide more light than old incandescent and fluorescent fixtures. Because LED tends to cost more than other options, I would make every

69

effort to purchase them when they are on sale. The same is true for purchasing LED light bulbs to place in existing lighting fixtures.

You may have to add some recessed can lighting or drop fixture lighting in the kitchen as well. My model was to always make the kitchen and baths more well-lit than they had been at the time of acquisition.

Seventeen. Carpet.

Carpet padding is less expensive per square yard than most carpet is. And good quality padding can make a lesser quality and less expensive carpeting seem more plush and expensive. Obviously, you cannot put cheap carpet into an expensive property; you must attempt to match the cost of the property with the quality of the carpeting. This is where an experienced carpet provider and installer can be extremely helpful to you.

To find a good carpet installer you could ask the management of a large apartment complex who they use to install carpet in their units, when carpet needs to be replaced, or if you join an investor's group like Chicago Creative Investors Association, you could ask other members who they use to install carpet.

A good installer will have a good idea about the grade of carpet you need for the particular property. He will measure your property and will determine how many square yards you will need for the property and will be able to show you samples from which to pick the color or

71

colors you want. However, the safest choice is to go neutral and avoid white and non-neutral colors.

On one occasion, our carpet installer saved us from a costly mistake. We had an offer on a townhome before we had completed the rehab and the Realtor who brought the buyer in told us that it was as good as assured that the buyer would get the financing. The buyer asked if she could make color choices on the carpet and we agreed. She chose black for the master bedroom and a green for the rest of the rooms. The day before the carpet was to be installed, we found out that the buyer would not be getting the mortgage because all of her information did not check out. We were able to get ahold of the carpet installer and have him bring neutral carpet instead of what the buyer had chosen. Because we had used his services on multiple occasions he did us a major favor and saved us the expense of having to replace the carpet at a future time.

I found out that he had his truck loaded with the black and green carpeting and removed that carpet and reloaded with neutral carpet as a favor to us. We did decide that we would never again allow a buyer to make any changes to what we were planning on doing, unless they were cash buyers or unless what they wanted was in harmony with what we were planning on doing anyway.

You definitely want a professional carpet installer who knows his trade well and who can present you with options.

As to whether or not you need to install new carpeting rather than having the old carpeting cleaned, that is a judgment call that you will have to make. I will say this, people who are behind in their payments and losing a home seldom are going to spend the money to have their carpet cleaned but only you can make the determination as to which way to go on the clean versus replace decision.

Eighteen.   HVAC (Heating, Ventilating, Air Conditioning).

A good HVAC man is worth his weight in gold. What do I mean by good? I mean one who will give you an honest appraisal of the equipment and system in your property and who will not try to sell you brand new equipment when your property does not need it.

Ten year old equipment may perform perfectly well and not need to be replaced. Maybe for the cost of having your technician perform a tune up on your equipment you can save thousands of dollars in not having to replace the equipment that is there.

New equipment is more efficient than older systems and can be vented with PVC piping directed out of the house and does not need to be directed to the chimney to vent flue gases, the quantity of which will be much lesser in newer, more efficient systems than in older, less efficient ones.

Because of federal regulations and energy guidelines new air conditioning equipment now uses R-410a, a refrigerant gas that is not only more expensive than R-22 which it replaced as of January 1, 2010 but which also does not have the ozone depleting effect, should it be leaked into the air. R-22 should be around to service older equipment until around 2024 and then only R-410a will be allowed to be sold. R-22 contributes to global warming, or at least ozone depletion, whereas R-410a does not—that might be something you want to consider. Air conditioning systems with R-22 can last up to 25 to 30 years because R-22 is very forgiving if not installed perfectly. If the installer is not very precise and allows a bit of moisture to get into the system with R-410a the system can fail much quicker because there is little forgiveness in equipment using R-410a.

The important point to remember is that if your Heating, Ventilation, and Air Conditioning contractor gives you and honest appraisal of the state of your equipment in the subject property, you might be able to avoid an unnecessary expenditure.

A furnace and heating equipment can last up to fifty percent longer than air conditioning equipment. Air conditioning components can typically last up to fifteen years. At ten years, issues of economic obsolescence may apply if the units were in your personal home; but in a property that is going to be sold, if they are in good condition, it may not make sound economic sense to replace them.

Another point to consider if the decision is made to replace existing equipment is if you are going to stay with the same type of system or go with another type. Twice I replaced gas boilers which supplied hot water heating to radiators and baseboard units throughout the property with gas forced air systems. In both instances the boilers were not well maintained, old, and very inefficient. By going with gas forced air it was easier to add central air conditioning to the properties. Probably at least a dozen other times, I replace gas forced air furnaces with newer, more efficient equipment. Radiators and beneath floor heating are technically superior heating systems, but are not always the type of thing that catches the eye of the potential buyer.

Nineteen. Avoiding New Roofs Unless Needed.

Usually, when you are looking at a property, you should be able to come to a decent conclusion about whether or not the property will need a new roof. There may be some times that you will find a problem in the attic that may necessitate replacing it or the roof looks good from the street but not so good when you see it from the other side of the property. Since most roofs are put on with permits, you should be able to ascertain the age of the roof that is present on the property at the time you purchase it. Unless there was a problem with the shingles themselves, which can happen, any roof less than ten years of age should be okay

In my opinion, a new roof adds nothing to your ability to resell the property because the buyers are not really going to pay it any attention unless there are noticeable flaws with it. It is a fairly pricey repair with little return in it. If I saw that the roof needed to be replaced, I would take that into account in determining what I was willing to pay for the property.

However, if you have to have a new roof put on the property, remember that the cleanest but most expensive option is to have a complete tear-off and then have the new shingles put on. The alternative is to have a second layer of shingles put over the existing ones. Most villages, cities, or counties allow two layers of shingles and some may even allow three layers. While a second layer is cheaper to you, the second layer will not last as long as it would have had you had the other shingles torn off first. Probably a second layer will only last eighty to eighty-five percent as long as the shingles would have lasted had there only been one layer. On the other hand, if you hire a licensed roofing contractor, he will stand behind his work (usually for at least ten years) and he may offer a warranty that is transferrable to the new owners, if the property is sold within a few years' time.

If you are going to have a new roof put on a property and you are not going to do the work yourself, get four or five estimates unless you know or are related to a roofer. In my experience the price you will be quoted by roofers can vary by as much as fifty percent. For example, if your lowest estimate is $4,000, then your highest estimate will be around $6,000.

In my twenty years of rehabbing, only twice have I ever had to replace a roof, one was on that property, which is shown on the cover of this book--everything in the property had to be replaced from bottom to top. The other time was on a home where a previous owner had replaced the roofing himself; and while it looked good from the ground, he had not placed felt paper or any barrier down first before shingling and he made another critical mistake in that he lined the tabs of the first two layers of shingles up exactly instead of having them overlapping. That allowed water to soak into the wood underlayment which in turn led to water destroying the studs in a section of wall about fifteen feet long. Several of the studs were reduced from three and a half inches to an inch or less.

If the property was not at the bottom of resell price pyramid, I might consider metal or even rubber roofing material. They are now making metal roofing that resembles shakes or shingles and are doing the same with rubber roofing, which is made out of recycled tires. The material costs for metal and rubber roofing is about twice that of asphalt shingles.

Twenty. Greening the Property.

If you have to replace a hot water heater, you might want to consider a tankless unit. While a tankless water heater is more costly than a regular gas or electric water heater it saves money by only heating water when there is a demand for it, which makes it very economical to operate fuel-wise as well as being very green. In fact, a tankless water heater will most likely pay for the difference in price within two to three years because of the reduction in fuel costs. Don't just do it for the sake of doing it; only consider doing it, if you need to replace the hot water heater.

Insulation helps green the property, but don't spend money just to do it. Only replace or install insulation when and if you have to open up walls. If you do wind up opening the walls, you might seriously want to consider insulating with closed cell foam insulation rather than fiberglass batts, which really are not all that energy efficient unless they are installed properly, which they frequently are not.

Closed cell foam insulation does not need to completely fill the cavity between the wall studs, but it is the most efficient type of insulation, it does not allow water or vapor permeation, and it will help to make the structure stronger. The house I put it in was built in the 1850s and had no modern insulation. There are several companies that sell closed cell insulating products, but I chose the Versi-Foam systems product for my project. To find out more about Versi-Foam and its products you can go to www.rhbfoamsystems.com

LED lighting or replacing incandescent or fluorescent light bulbs with led bulbs is the way to go nowadays because the bulbs will last for twenty-five years or considerably longer and they save sixty or more percent of electricity used by incandescent bulbs. I would suggest that you purchase led bulbs when they are sale because they are not cheap when compared to incandescent or compact fluorescent light bulbs.

If you need to replace windows, your best course of action is to replace existing windows with the best energy saving windows you can buy for the property, given the constraint of not over

82

improving the property. Even companies like Andersen Windows make units in several price points.

We generally installed ceiling fan lights in all bedrooms and some of the other rooms as well because they come in a wide variety of prices, can be energy saving, if used properly, and can help sell your property.

Furnaces, like hot water heaters, are more energy efficient today than they were in the near past. I would not replace a furnace just for the sake of replacing; however, if the property definitely needed a new furnace, you can get one that fits in the price range of the property you have. For instance, smaller homes can use smaller, less expensive furnaces while larger homes are going to require larger furnaces and larger air conditioning units or even multiple units.

Faucets that require less water flow to operate are definitely in the green category and they save the future homeowner money on their water bills. The same is true for newer dishwashers and clothes washers, if those appliance need to be replaced.

Since almost all toilets sold in the United States today have tanks that hold no more than 1.4 gallons of water, just installing a new toilet is not that much of a greening project unless the toilets being replaced are the old 3 plus gallon models. But many new toilets have two options for flushing: one where less water is used if only urine is being flushed and one which empties the tank, if solids are being flushed.

If you have to put a new roof on the property and you have the money to spend, you could always have a rubber roof put on the property. Rubber roofing, as previously mentioned, is made out of recycled automobile tires. Could you get any greener than that? It will cost you though because rubber shingles are in the same price range as metal roofing.

If "green" is an ultimate goal for a specific project, you can go as far as to using countertop materials that would be less impactful on the environment. Bamboo, recycled paper, recycled glass, or scrap metal countertops all fit into that category.

There are many ways to green a property and those things can be touted when trying to resell the property because most potential buyers like those features and like thinking that they are purchasing a "green" property.

Twenty-one. Odds and Ends.

You want to add a bathroom in a basement or in an area with a cement slab underneath, what can you do? The traditional way of handling this task has been to jackhammer the cement slab and lay pipe to connect into the sewer system somewhere under the cement, which can be a huge task if you want to install a bathroom at one end of the property and the sewer connections for the property are at the other end of the property.

The modern option is to purchase one of the Saniflow (www.saniflow.com) products and construct your proposed bathroom without any major cement demolition. The basis of a Saniflow system is a toilet connected to a macerating pump to which two other units (sink, tub, or shower) can be connected and all of the waste and waste water can be pumped overhead into the sewer pipes.

Once, we took an attached one-car garage and converted it into a bedroom and a utility room. Since the home was on a slab and we did not want to jackhammer enough concrete to run plumbing pipes twenty-five feet to tie into the existing sewer pipes, we dug a pit to hold a sump pump and directed all of the waste water from the utility sink and the clothes washer into the pit. The pump then sent the waste water up to the ceiling and through the ceiling to an interior wall where the pipes came down and were directed to the existing sewer pipe.

For most of the homes that had decks, it was necessary to power wash and re-stain the deck. One property had a second story deck built out over the roof of an addition. The wood on that deck was too far gone to simply power wash and re-stain, so we replaced the original wood decking with Azek, a capped PVC product, because Azek is impervious to water and because someone had replaced the original railing system with white PVC and the Azek matched it so that the entirety looked better to the eye.

When it comes to decking material, there is pressure treated and other soft woods, wood plastic composite, capped wood plastic composite, capped PVC, and NyloDeck, which is made from one hundred percent recycled carpet fiber. It is manufactured to have the look of natural wood. The real wood options are the least expensive materials to begin with but over time, due to the power washing, re-staining, and replacing a board every now and then, it becomes the most expensive option.

Wood garage doors and wood front doors with sidelights are impressive looking but they have to be maintained annually or semi-annually. In the seven year old home that I have mentioned previously, the three wood garage doors were completely shot because they had never been maintained. Rather than replacing them with wood, we replaced them with insulated metal doors. The front door and the sidelights had problems as well because of a lack of maintenance. We re-stained the door and the sidelights but it was not sufficient to get rid of the problems that had resulted from a lack of maintenance for seven years. Instead of replacing the door and the sidelights, I found a fancy storm door with sidelights that covered all of the original wood and which eliminated water and air penetration. Because the storm door and sidelights system cost only about one-fifth of the price of a new wood door and sidelights, it was not only an improvement but an economical one as well.

When you have finished with one part of the property but are still working in other areas, if you want to contain the dust you are creating so that you do not have to do thorough cleaning again, you may want to use a ZipWall dust barrier system. You can check out how easy it is to install and use it and where you can purchase it by going to the ZipWall web page (www.zipwall.com)

Speaking of controlling dust, RotoZip is manufacturing a roto saw with a dust vault (think built-in vacuum). The dust vault of the tool is claimed to reduce dust and debris by 90%. If you want to check the tool out you can go to the RotoZip page (www.rotozip.com)

One of the first things you should do upon taking possession of the property is to go to the electrical box and make certain that you know which breakers control appliances, lighting, and outlets around the property. In one two story house, we had difficulty figuring out what

89

controlled the lighting and outlets on the second floor because we could not seem to be able to isolate the breaker. What we found after diligently searching around was that, at one time, there had been an electrical fire in the attic. That fire has caused the insulation around the wires to be melted off which led to some of the wiring to be fused together. Since the wiring had been laying on top of each other, the heat from the wiring had most likely been the cause of the fire itself. The previous homeowners were lucky that the fire had not caused more damage and also lucky that the system had continue working. It is not uncommon to find evidence of small fires happening in attics, especially in older homes.

Twenty-two. Health and Safety Issues.

Safety would include installing working smoke detectors (including some hardwired in the electrical system with backup batteries), carbon monoxide detectors, a fire extinguisher for the kitchen and maybe another area in the property, safety covers for electrical outlets (in case small children might be living in the property) that are low on the walls or in the floor., proper lighting, and perhaps a collapsible, wall cavity mounted ladder for emergency exiting the second story of a two-story home in case of a fire.

Anti-scald valves on the tub/shower fixtures in the bathrooms would be included in this as well. Making certain that there are hand rails for every set of stairs in the property; and if there are hand rails there already ensuring that they are securely fastened to wall studs.

Every exterior door should have both a handset lock as well as a deadbolt lock. This goes for the door between the house and the attached garage, if the property includes an attached garage. All windows should either be of a type that does not open or, if opening, have some type of device for locking them and preventing easy access from the outside by potential robbers or vandals.

Depending on how much the property would resell for and whether you have to open up the ceilings, you might consider installing a sprinkler system for putting out fires. There are a couple of companies that manufactured systems using plastic piping.

Any over/range in the property should be accompanied by a property secured anti-tip device. If any new refrigerator you purchase for the property comes with an anti-falling restraint be sure to install it per the instructions. These safety features can be touted when the property is listed for resell.

Twenty-three. Safety and Deterrence.

In lower price range properties in high crime areas, we installed burglar bars, which could be opened by residents needing to exit the property in case of a fire.

We bought a fairly inexpensive security system comprised of motion detecting sensors connected to an audible alarm. It provided us with some peace of mind and one time it even scared a potential burglar away. Before we had finished installing burglar bars on a property, someone pried open a window and attempted to enter the property; the motion detectors must have caught the action and the alarm went off and scared the burglar away.

Like I said, the security system was inexpensive and it was easily transported to new properties when they were acquired. Today there are systems like Ring and Doorbot, both of which are under $200, that allow you to see who is at your front door or near it. The equipment will send you video via Wi-Fi to your smart phone or tablet and allow you to speak with the person or persons even if you are hundreds or thousands of

93

miles away. I suspect that there are many other pieces of equipment that you can acquire that will help you protect your property. A system like either of them could even be used to keep track of showings by Realtors as well. Modern wireless technology is making it easier to protect your property and you should take complete advantage of it.

I installed a Westinghouse Beyond Icebox 12.1 inch Flipscreen under cabinet television and computer system in the kitchen of a pinnacle of the pyramid property. It could play DVDs, CDs, or MP3 discs, it allowed one to watch favorite television shows, the morning news, or cooking shows. It had internet connectivity so one could send emails, pull up favorite recipes, check one's favorite sites, and came with a dishwasher safe keyboard and remote. By attaching a video camera to the Icebox, one could see who was at the front door, watch a sleeping infant, or keep an eye on the kids in the backyard while they were playing.

Technology is advancing so rapidly that you have to keep checking to discover what new and functional products are on the market to provide

94

more security for your properties. The Westinghouse system that I installed in the one property that was state-of-the-art ten to fifteen years ago is probably a dinosaur today.

Twenty-four. Garage Door Opener and Remotes.

It is very difficult to sell a property without a garage, unless you are in the lower end of the market. I have sold five properties that had no garage: two were in a townhome complex where no one had a garage, one was a complete rehab where the attached garage was converted to living space, one was the property that had two houses on the same parcel, and one was a property that had been a three unit rental that we reduced to two units.

The property with two houses on the same parcel was sold to a nonprofit community organization; that group was committed to decreasing density in that city so they tore down one of the houses and built a detached garage where it had been. Fortunately for them, there had been a driveway between the two houses, which made it easier for them to do that.

The three unit rental was reduced to two units (one on the main floor of the property and one upstairs) because we realized that one of the units on the main floor would never be conforming to new City codes. It had a shower in an alcove off of a bedroom, a toilet in what became a closet, and the lavatory sink and the kitchen sink were the same—three bathroom fixtures in three separate rooms. That property had no garage but it did have an extra wide driveway and sufficient space to park six vehicles.

If there is a garage, there also needs to be a garage door opener on every garage door; and those units need to be functioning and have and have at least two remote opener units available. The garage door opener does not have to be new—it does have to be functioning. Additionally, there has to be a minimum of two functioning remotes available for each garage door opener, if it is located on a single car garage and more if it is a two car garage.

If you have an existing garage door opener that you do not need to replace but you do not have sufficient remotes, you can often find remote openers for existing units either in retail stores or online. If you cannot find remotes that will operate the existing garage door opener, then you are probably going to have to replace the garage door opener itself.

At the property which had a detached four car garage with two garage doors and openers, I was able to purchase a total of four remotes for each garage door opener and, as a result, did not have to replace either opener. Another property had an attached three car garage and while I had to replace all three garage doors, the openers were all in very good condition and I was able to secure enough remotes so that I had a total of six of them as well as a hardwired button to open and close each of the units next to the door from the garage into the house.

You may say to yourself that many people do not even park their cars in their garages or that they may put one vehicle in a two car garage and use the remainder of the space for storage. It does not really matter because buyers have a mental image of how they would like things to be. It is the same with decks that seldom get used and fireplaces in which they never have a fire. The perception has greater value than the actual reality of how they will live.

Twenty-five. Blacktopping a Gravel Driveway.

A completely gravel driveway is not very desirable. You might be able to get away with it if it is in a neighborhood where that is the prevailing norm or if there is enough garage space to park at least two vehicles inside of it.

In the property with a four car detached garage there was a cement pad capable of holding four full size cars and vans in front of the garage. In front of that for another car-length was gravel. Because there was some drop off from the cement to the gravel, we had sufficient gravel trucked in to make it more uniform and to get rid of the bump.

One property had a rather lengthy gravel driveway (around one hundred twenty-five feet or more) leading up to a one car attached garage. Because at least one vehicle would have to be parked outside, if the buyer had two or more vehicles, we had that driveway blacktopped. Gravel driveways can be quite messy when it rains or there is snow on the driveway. In this instance having the driveway blacktopped really

99

helped to sell the property to a new buyer, especially because the cement pad in front of the garage was not sufficient to contain a vehicle.

Other than the examples provided, I have never had to do anything to a driveway. That is not to say that they were all perfect or that none of the others had gravel rather than being blacktopped or cemented. The others either had sufficient garage space or paved space to park on and no risk of tracking a mess into the property.

Twenty-six. Insect and Vermin Free.

Insects and vermin are just nicer sounding words than roaches and mice or rats. You could also include ants, wasps, and termites in the insect category and having squirrels and raccoons in the attic or garage in the vermin category. Although Japanese Beetles do not invade residential property they can be devastating to plant life in the yard, and if there is a particularly large number of them invading your property, you will probably want to purchase a Japanese Beetle trap or two to place in the yard of the property.

Before you go the route of hiring professional exterminators to take care of roaches or other insects, do what you can yourself to rid the property of such pests. You can purchase products at the big home center chains or big box stores that should allow you to get those problems under control. One property was so roach infested that I set off seven 'bombs' inside the property over a period of a few weeks. After the program was completed there was no sign of any living roaches.

Now, should you find a termite infestation in your property, I am not certain that there is any do-it-yourself solution; in that case I believe that you will have to hire a termite exterminator, who will have to tent your property in order to get rid of the infestation.

Mice and rats are a nuisance that you should be able to eliminate with products and traps purchased at a big box store. I have been lucky in that I have never had to deal with rats, squirrels, or raccoons in a property. If you have squirrels or raccoons in an attic or garage, you can either purchase a 'have a heart' trap, catch them, and release them in a forest preserve or hire a guy who will do that for you.

I have had mice in a couple of properties. In one we caught twenty-seven of them. These were not traps from which the mice would be leaving alive. One property where we had discovered mice was prone to having them seek shelter inside in the late fall. In addition to leaving a few traps inside, I took a more proactive position by taking four twenty inch lengths of two inch diameter PVC pipe and placing a cap at each end. I then drilled a 5/8 inch hole in each cap and put a commonly purchased mouse and rat bait inside. The holes meant that only mice or something similarly sized would be able to get inside the pipe and be able to access the bait. The pipes needed to have their contents refilled about every three weeks but it did solve the problem for as long as I owned the property.

Nothing can deter a sale faster than a potential buyer seeing insects or vermin in the property or signs of them being present. So, it is definitely in your best interest to rid your property of these pests.

Twenty-seven. Curb Appeal.

Planting vegetation, such as trees, bushes, and flowers can greatly approve the curb appeal of the property. Sometimes, curb appeal can be a major factor in the reselling of the property and in getting the best price for the property. On the Live Well Network's Fix This Yard Co-hosts Amy Devers and Alan Luxmore demonstrate how improving the curb appeal of a property can significantly raise the appraised value of the home.

While I normally endorse taking the inexpensive route on most purchases, you may have to spend a bit more on some things. Say for instance you decide to purchase some arbor vitae trees for the property. Do not buy all twelve inch trees—get some four, five, and even six foot specimens to make the landscaping appear more mature.

Because buyers are going to notice the front of the property and the side that the driveway is on more so than the back or the side opposite the driveway, you may be able to transplant some mature vegetation, if it is attractive and in good condition, from elsewhere in the yard to the front of the property.

As far as bushes go, burning bush plants are impressive, particularly in the fall. If you are in doubt about what to purchase, ask the garden expert at whatever place you purchase your plants which varieties are particularly hardly in your climate, are easy to care for, and which look best in either the spring or the fall.

I purchased almost all of my vegetation from home centers, like Menard's, Lowe's, and Home Depot and I would purchase items when they were on sale. That way I got the biggest bang for my dollars.

There are going to be times when you may not have to worry about vegetation as an aid in curb appeal because you may buy the property in the fall, after the growing season, and may be able to resell it in the winter or very early spring, before you can really undertake any planting. If you do purchase a property in the early spring, you should include the planting of vegetation as a part of your rehab process.

When purchasing flowers, my advice is to avoid annuals—unless you want to fill a planter near the front or side doors. Perennials, which come back every year are a better investment because they make the potentials buyers feel that they will not have to do as much in order to maintain the landscaping.

A nice eight to twelve foot tree can be impressive if it is placed well and is a shade or fruit-bearing variety.

Twenty-eight. Keeping Up Appearances.

Whether you do the work yourself or hire a lawn service to do it, you should maintain the appearance of the lawn and the property during the grass growing season. Additionally, you should either rake the leaves or have them raked in the fall.

This not only makes the property more presentable should potential buyers drive through the area but it will also make most of your neighbors happy that you are maintaining the property, which might lead them to telling friends or relatives looking for a property in that area about your property. So, there can be multiple benefits from keeping up appearances.

Associated with this is ridding the property of any trash or junk in the yard and making sure that there is no buildup of trash in the yard.

Trimming trees and bushes can fall either in this category or in the curb appeal category. Wherever you want to consider it, it provides a sense of care that subconsciously the potential buyers pick up on. If the sidewalk leading to the front door of the house is blocked by an overgrown bush, you really need to either have that bush trimmed or replaced by a bush that is of acceptable size.

Twenty-nine. Never Get Greedy,

If your Realtor, who you like and, more importantly, really trust, tells you that the property you are rehabbing will sell for $220,000 don't start thinking that because you have put everything new inside of it that you can get $250,000. You start doing things like that and you are going to be holding properties a lot longer than you need to be.

Now, I can look you in the face, figuratively speaking, and tell you that even though I have violated that principle three times myself; and done so successfully. One was the house that was burnt by the previous owner. I figured that since everything was completely new except for the foundation that I could get more than anything else in the neighborhood had. I was right and the offer came in within two weeks of being listed. My favorite one was a small townhome in a complex where most resells sold in the $60.000s and a few managed to eke into the $70,000s. I wanted to list it at $83,000 even though my partner and the Realtor both thought that I was nuts. We got a full price offer on the second day of the listing.

109

Why was I so confident? Because I am a really great designer of kitchens and baths. In these units, they had a very decently sized kitchen/dining room space that ran along the back width of the units, but the kitchen were basically galley kitchen with refrigerators, sinks, and stoves all along one wall, which did not leave either a lot of counter space or a lot of cabinet space. In a couple of units, someone added what amounted to a long island running parallel to the existing kitchen cabinets and appliances. I decided to block off one of the two doorways going into the rest of the unit in order to create a big "L" shaped kitchen with more than triple the counter space and cabinet space and moved the stove to where the doorway had been. It was a woman's dream and I figured that we could break the record because of it. A few years later, I was able to obtain an even larger unit in the complex. I did the same thing to the kitchen and once again—only this time I moved the refrigerator to the end of the new part of the "L" and this time we shattered the record in the complex by even more because prices had gone up since I had owned the first one and this was one of the eight larger units in the complex.

Other than those exceptions, I always heeded the Realtor's advice.

That is not entirely true because four times I sold properties without a Realtor. Once for a quick $10,000 profit to a flipper who thought I was nuts for selling it so cheaply to him; but I had two other properties that I was working on simultaneously, and as it turned out I made the right decision. Another was when I sold my interest in the foreclosure that a flipper and I bought together to him for a quick $25,000 profit. Another time, I purchased a foreclosure for $13,100 and sold it to a neighbor who wanted to use it as a rental—all we had to do was clean it up and install a new furnace and hot water heater, which combined did not even cost $600 at that time. I agreed to sell it to him for $47,500 with no selling expenses on my part. At the closing his attorney tried to make me pay prorations and I told him that he could forget about that because my deal with his client, which was in writing, was that I would leave the closing with a check for $47.500 and that I would simply walk away from the closing if the check from the title company was for anything

111

less than that. Finally, I sold two properties on the same parcel to an organization that was looking to decrease density in the City of Elgin. I only sold it to them because both parcels shared the same city water and sewer system and I could not find an economical and under the radar way of separating them; all I had to do was clean up the property and made a quick $30,000 profit. I could have gotten more from them but I wanted a quick sale and closing. I might easily have been able to get double that from the organization but I wanted them to realize that they were getting such a good deal that they had to accept my offer.

I once bought a foreclosure primarily because I knew it had been under contract at the time of the foreclosure sale. I knew the outside of the property needed to be painted for the bank to approve the buyer's mortgage. It was almost too late in the year to be painting outside but we did it anyway and listed it right away hoping we would attract the would-be buyer back to look at the property. Had that not worked we would have had to do more work on the property but then we could have listed it for a higher price.

Luck was on our side, the buyer came back the second day of the listing and made the same offer that he and the previous owner had agreed to before the foreclosure sale. We accepted the offer and made a quick $28,000 profit.

On one of the first rehabs that I ever did, I had both a work partner and a money partner. We thought we would make an attempt to sell it ourselves as a "For Sale by Owner." We had an open house one Sunday and before it was to begin, the three of us sat in the kitchen and agreed to a price that we would accept on the property. A woman came through the property with her husband, it was her dream house, and they made an offer which was exactly what we had agreed to accept. The money partner spoke with the woman and her husband, since he was handling the negotiation, and instead of accepting the offer, he attempted to get them to sweeten the pot by obtaining some additional funds from her father.

The deal fell completely and irretrievably apart because the one partner got greedy. As so often happens when you get greedy, we got nothing or far less than we wanted. We wound up listing

113

with a Realtor, it took a few months to sell, and when it did, we netted $18,000 less than we would have netted had the money partner not gotten greedy.

Thirty. Location, Location, Location.

Perhaps this should have been in the book earlier, but here it is. When I was a Realtor, we had a saying, "Location, location, location." Basically, it means that where the property is located is often more relevant to its ability to sell than anything else about the property. This does not even take into consideration things like the perceived quality of the area's school district or whether the property is on city services versus being on well and septic,

A two story home in a neighborhood of similar homes should sell more easily than a two story home in a neighborhood of ranch or one story homes. It is usually more difficult to sell a residential property that is next to a factory than it is to sell one in a completely residential neighborhood. A residential property on a very busy street or highway is more difficult to sell than one located on a low traffic volume residential street.

There is nothing you can do about the location of the property after you have purchased it, but location should definitely enter into you considerations about purchasing the property before you have purchased it. If the price you can purchase it for is exceptional, then it still might be well worth it for you to go ahead, but be aware that it will probably take you longer to resell the property after you have finished the rehabbing of it.

Thirty-one. The Time Value of Money.

What is your time worth? I do not think that there is a universal answer to this question; I think that this is a question that everyone must decide for themselves.

Remember the home I sold to a neighbor where I walked away from the closing with a check for $47,500? Many might say why not go ahead and rehab the property because you would walk away with more afterward. That is true. But the home really needed a lot of work to make it sellable and probably the highest sale price for it would have been $82,000. Now, the way I calculate it between the rehab time and the time on market to sell it, I would have had it on my hands for another eight months and after paying the real estate commission, seller closing expenses, and materials costs involved with the rehab, I would have been lucky, extremely lucky to clear another $16,000. I would have done just that had I not had another option; but in this case I felt the additional $16,000 was not worth an additional eight months of my time.

When I spent the better part of three days attempting to clean all of the grease from an over/range and was still not able to get it completely clean; and would not have been able to do so without taking the oven door completely apart because there was grease trapped between the inner and outer panels of glass in the door. That was when I decided that my time which could have been better used for other rehab projects in the property than cleaning used appliances. Also, at the time, I could pick up a new oven/range appropriate for the price of the townhome for approximately three hundred dollars. The new oven/range could be featured in the listing for the property and appealed to a buyer more so than a used one.

Perhaps you do not think that your time has much value; and, if that is the case, then you can simply pay no attention to this chapter. On the other hand, you might want to give serious consideration to ways in which you can maximize the value of your time. Throughout this book, I have provided several examples of selling property without doing a rehab on the property. Each one of those could have been

118

more profitable had the property been rehabbed but then there would have been at least six, and possibly more, months added to the duration and the extra profit to be made did not seem worth the extra time.

Thirty-two. About the Cover.

The two pictures on the cover are before and after pictures of the same property, in case you could not tell. The quality of the before picture is not very good and that is because it was taken from a Polaroid shot of the property. It had brown wooden, vertical siding that would have looked better on a barn. The windows were drafty and the garage door was greatly deteriorated.

 This is one of my favorites because it was one of the most complete makeovers. I think that the only thing that was not replaced was the toilet and that was because it mounted to the wall rather than the floor and it was not that easy that it was in pretty good condition.

The house was purchased at a foreclosure auction. The plaintiff's bid was for less than its judgement because it knew that the property was in bad shape. It had sat vacant over the winter and had not been properly winterized; as a result the joints in the copper piping supplying hot water to the baseboard radiators had separated and there were splits in some of the piping itself.

120

All the walls were opened up and insulation was put in the cavities. All the windows were replaced with new energy efficient models. Even though the windows were new, they were not that expensive compared to top of the line models. New siding, new roof, and a fireplace was installed (you can see the metal chimney coming through the roof in the after picture). We stripped off the old shingles, but hired a roofer to put the new shingles on the property. We installed the gas fireplace in the living room/family room combination because it was such a big room and we wanted to give it a focal point. With all new cabinets, countertops, and appliances the kitchen became a large gourmet, eat in kitchen. The washer and dryer location that had been in the kitchen were moved into a new utility room at the back of what had been the attached garage. The washer and dryer placed in the new utility room were not the old ones but new inexpensive models. The front of the former attached garage became the largest bedroom or whatever else the buyers wanted to use it for and the old baseboard heating system was replaced with gas forced air heating, which allowed for the installation of central air conditioning.

About the Author.

Jay Thomas is the pseudonym of an Amazon best-selling non-fiction author.

He has a Bachelor's degree from the University of Dayton and a Master's degree in Planning from the University of Cincinnati.

The author spent over twenty years buying, rehabbing, and reselling residential properties. Previous to that, he worked for quasi-governmental, non-profit agencies, had a bakery in a mall, ran a major metropolitan newspaper delivery agency, and was a Realtor and Broker Associate.

www.ingramcontent.com/pod-product-compliance
Lightning Source LLC
Chambersburg PA
CBHW051326170526
45166CB00002B/697